Landmark Events in American History

Fort Sumter:
The Civil War Begins

Michael V. Uschan

WORLD ALMANAC® LIBRARY

To the students of General Mitchell Elementary School

Please visit our web site at: www.worldalmanaclibrary.com
For a free color catalog describing World Almanac® Library's list of high-quality books and multimedia programs, call 1-800-848-2928 (USA) or 1-800-387-3178 (Canada). World Almanac® Library's fax: (414) 332-3567.

Library of Congress Cataloging-in-Publication Data

Uschan, Michael V., 1948-
    Fort Sumter: the Civil War begins / by Michael V. Uschan.
      p. cm. — (Landmark events in American history)
    Includes bibliographical references and index.
    ISBN 0-8368-5395-4 (lib. bdg.)
    ISBN 0-8368-5423-3 (softcover)
    1. Fort Sumter (Charleston, S.C.)—Siege, 1861—Juvenile literature. 2. United States—History—Civil War, 1861-1865—Causes—Juvenile literature. 3. Charleston (S.C.)—History—Civil War, 1861-1865—Juvenile literature. I. Title. II. Series.
    E471.1.U83   2004
    973.7'31—dc22   2004045965

First published in 2005 by
World Almanac® Library
330 West Olive Street, Suite 100
Milwaukee, WI 53212 USA

Copyright © 2005 by World Almanac® Library.

Produced by Discovery Books
Editor: Sabrina Crewe
Designer and page production: Sabine Beaupré
Photo researcher: Sabrina Crewe
Maps and diagrams: Stefan Chabluk
World Almanac® Library editorial direction: Mark J. Sachner
World Almanac® Library editor: Gini Holland
World Almanac® Library art direction: Tammy West
World Almanac® Library production: Jessica Morris

Photo credits: Corbis: pp. 4, 11, 12, 15, 17, 18, 19, 20, 23, 28, 30, 31, 33, 35, 36, 38, 39, 40, 41, 43; Library of Congress: pp. 14, 37; National Park Service/Fort Sumter National Monument: pp. 32, 42; North Wind Picture Archives: cover, pp. 5, 6, 7, 8, 9, 10, 13, 21, 22, 25, 26, 27, 29, 34.

Printed in Canada

1 2 3 4 5 6 7 8 9 08 07 06 05 04

Contents

Introduction

Fort Sumter, where the Civil War began, is still standing in Charleston Harbor. It is now a national monument.

An Attack in Charleston Harbor

In 1861, the United States War Department was in the process of building a large structure called Fort Sumter on an island in Charleston Harbor, South Carolina. Although the fort's outside walls had been erected, some interior structures were still incomplete.

At 4:30 A.M. on April 12, 1861, cannonballs began raining down on Fort Sumter. The cannons were fired by soldiers of the **Confederate** States of America, also known as the Confederacy. After thirty-four hours of fighting, the small **Union** force inside Fort Sumter surrendered to the Confederate army.

The Beginning of the Civil War

The Confederate states included South Carolina and other southern states that no longer wanted to be part of the United States. In 1861, there were several reasons why the northern and southern regions of the United States were in conflict. The most severe dispute between the two parts of the nation was over slavery. Many people in the northern states believed slavery was wrong and should be ended, while white Southerners wanted the right to own African-American slaves.

The assault on Fort Sumter began the **Civil War**, a bloody and tragic conflict that devastated the nation for four years. It split the **North** and **South** and killed many thousands of soldiers and **civilians**. The Union victory over the Confederacy in 1865 did finally bring an end to slavery, but the cost in human life was immense.

BUILT FROM THE RUINS.

This banner was displayed during the convention in Charleston at which South Carolina decided to leave the Union. The banner shows a new "southern republic" built from the ruins of the United States.

The Human Cost of the Civil War

Due to the lack of accurate records, historians can only estimate how many Union and Confederate soldiers died in the Civil War. One estimate is that more than 650,000 Americans died—about 380,000 Northerners and 270,000 Southerners. However, some historians believe the death toll may have been as high as 700,000. That number does not include the many civilians who died during fighting that took place in or near their communities. In addition, hundreds of thousands of soldiers were wounded, many of them maimed for life by the loss of limbs or other horrific injuries.

Chapter 1

North and South

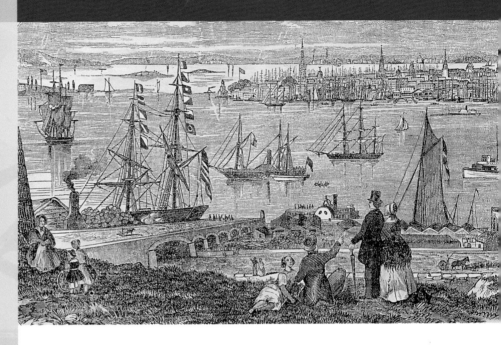

The harbors of the northeastern United States were important outlets for importing and exporting goods. This is New York Harbor in the 1850s.

The United States in the 1800s

In the first half of the nineteenth century, the United States America changed rapidly. Not only did it expand geographica first into central North America and then to the West, but population grew by leaps and bounds. In 1800, there were ab 6 million people living in the United States; by 1860, that fig had jumped to well over 30 million.

The North and South in 1860: A Comparison

	North	South
Population	22,700,000	9,000,000
(figure for the South includes 3.5–4 million slaves)		
Percentage of people living in cities and towns	26%	10%
Number of factories	110,000	18,000
Number of industrial workers	1,300,000	110,000
Percentage of cloth manufactured in United States	94%	3%
Percentage of iron manufactured in United States	93%	7%

In the mid-1800s, the United States was mostly an agricultural society, although the percentage of city dwellers grew from 6 percent to 20 percent between 1800 and 1860. Most of this urban growth, however, took place in the northern states, also called "the North."

The North

In the 1700s, when the states were still colonies under British rule, the North had developed shipping, fishing, and other business interests. An important part of the northern **economy** was based on trade with countries in Europe, and this flourishing trade created large cities such as New York, Boston, and Philadelphia.

In the 1800s—when mass production of goods in factories began and canals and railroads brought new forms of transportation—the economy and cities of the North expanded rapidly. The manufacturing industries, producing everything from textiles to parts for machinery, brought great wealth to the northeastern states. Farming of crops such as wheat and corn continued to flourish in the North as well, and agricultural production grew in the mid-1800s with the invention of new, efficient machines that could do the work of many laborers. Over the years, the demand for farm laborers slowly decreased, but the need for factory workers grew dramatically.

Much of the nation's wealth came from the textile mills of the Northeast. These looms for weaving cotton threads into cloth were used in the 1800s and have been preserved at the Boott Cotton Mills in Lowell, Massachusetts.

The South

Things were very different in the southern states, or "the South." There were many fewer railroads and canals, only a handful of large cities, and not many factories. The economy in southern states remained firmly rooted in agriculture, with the warm climate allowing for large-scale

production of cotton and tobacco. The demand for these produ
in the North and in Europe was huge, and tobacco and cotton pl:
tations frequently covered thousands of acres of land. Farmers a
produced food crops, but most manufactured goods were bou
from the North.

Another huge difference between the economies and cultu
of North and South was due to slavery. While slavery had be
abolished in nearly all parts of the North in the course of the ea
to mid-1800s, it continued to flourish in the South. There,
economy of the region and the wealth of plantation own
depended greatly on the forced free labor of slaves.

Differences Cause Conflict

The economies of the two regions, while separate, depended
each other. This fact unfortunately served to cause conflict a
resentment rather than bring unity. Cotton was the United Sta
major export, and cotton was grown in the South. The cotton tra
however, was controlled by Northerners because it was in
North that shippers, bankers, and textile merchants were bas
This fact caused great bitterness in the South.

Because of the slavery system, a handful of plantation owners in the South became immensely rich while most Southerners remained poor. Slaves received no pay for their work because they were owned, not employed.

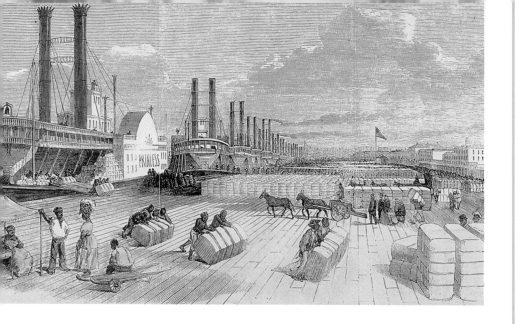

Cotton came from farms and plantations all over the South to a few main southern ports, such as New Orleans, shown here. The bales of cotton were then shipped to the North.

The way in which the two areas of the United States developed economically divided them on political issues, such as the payment of taxes. For example, Southerners were furious about new taxes introduced in 1828 and 1832 on manufactured goods. They believed the tax system favored northern states where most manufactured items were made; Southerners had to pay the taxes when they bought the items. After South Carolina declared the taxes illegal and other southern states protested them, Congress reduced the taxes, but the issue had widened the growing rift between the North and South.

Attitudes in North and South

By 1860, residents of the North and South were also firmly divided by their attitudes and hostility toward each other. Northerners looked down on Southerners because they generally had less education as well as a "backward" agricultural economy. Southerners resented Northerners for being overly concerned with making money in any way possible and generally having a superior attitude toward the South. An editor of a Georgia newspaper declared northern states were populated by "greasy mechanics, filthy [businessmen and] small farmers" who were unsuited to live in a "society fitted for well-bred gentlemen." A New York newspaper claimed Southerners knew little about "thrift, cleanliness, and usefulness, honesty, decency, or common humanity." Above all, attitudes and beliefs about slavery caused a divide that grew from disagreement to outright conflict.

Thoroughly Distinct
"There exists a great mistake in supposing that the people of the United States are, or ever have been, one people. On the contrary, never did the sun shine on two people as thoroughly distinct as the people of the North and South."

Robert Barnwell Rhett, resident of Charleston, South Carolina, the New York Tribune, November 10, 1860

Chapter 2

Slavery and the Abolition Movement

Africans were brought to North America on slave ships such as the one shown here. Many thousands of people traveled in horrific conditions on the slave ships before the trade was banned in 1808.

Slavery in North America

The first slaves were brought to the British colonies in No America in 1619, when a group of Africans were brought to colony of Jamestown, Virginia, and sold to the English sett there. It was not until the 1700s that slavery really took hold, by the time the United States was founded in 1776, slavery was accepted practice. Early presidents George Washington a Thomas Jefferson both owned slaves.

In 1808, a law was passed in Congress that banned the imp of new slaves. The number of slaves continued to grow, however

African-American slaves in the South had children who automatically became slaves themselves. By 1850, there were an estimated 3.2 million African Americans in the United States, nearly all of them slaves. In South Carolina and Mississippi, there were more black people than white. Until 1850, slaves could still be bought and sold in Washington, D.C., the nation's capital.

Abolitionists

In the first half of the nineteenth century, the difficult issue of slavery increasingly divided the United States. Many more people in the North became convinced slavery should be outlawed altogether because they believed it was immoral. The antislavery campaigners were called **abolitionists**—they infuriated white Southerners, who believed the South needed slave labor in order to remain strong economically.

In their campaigning, abolitionists called attention to and protested the way slaves were treated. Men, women, and children who were slaves had no rights, and their owners thought of them simply as property. They were bought and sold in markets like animals and could be whipped or killed if they displeased their masters. Slaves worked twelve to sixteen hours a day in the fields and often owned no possessions other than the clothes they wore.

Victim of Injustice

"What, to the American slave, is your Fourth of July? I answer: a day that reveals to him, more than all other days in the year, the gross injustice and cruelty to which he is the constant victim. To him, your celebration is a sham."

Abolitionist and former slave
Frederick Douglass, July 4, 1841

11

Slave or Free?

Some southern whites realized slavery was cruel. Mary Chesnut was the wife of James Chesnut, a South Carolina U.S. senator in the 1850s. In her diary, she called slavery "this hated institution" and declared, "God forgive us, but ours is a monstrous system and

Escaping from Slavery

In 1838, Frederick Douglass boarded a train in Baltimore, Maryland, as a slave. When Douglass reached Philadelphia, Pennsylvania, he was able to live as a free man, and in 1847 he purchased his freedom for $150. Douglass was one of many thousands of blacks who escaped from slavery by fleeing to the North. From about 1830 to 1860, many thousands of people escaped on what was called the "Underground Railroad." It was not a real railroad, but a network of hiding places and secret routes organized to help smuggle slaves from the South to the North. The heroic Harriet Tubman, who escaped from slavery herself in 1849, was one of more than three thousand Underground Railroad workers. She went south fifteen times to help slaves escape and took an estimated three hundred people to freedom.

Escaped slaves, helped by Underground Railroad volunteers, arrive at a safe "station" on their way to the North.

In 1856, proslavery and antislavery groups began warring openly in Kansas Territory, where both sides set up territorial **legislatures**. The violence was so bad that the territory was named "Bleeding Kansas."

wrong." Most Southerners, however, were absolutely determined to protect the institution of slavery.

As white Americans headed west to settle on new lands, new conflicts appeared. Southerners wanted slavery to be made legal in new **U.S. territories** and states, while Northerners wanted to keep slavery from spreading. The Compromise of 1850 settled several years of political fighting. Under the agreement, California was admitted into the Union as a free state (meaning a state where no slavery was allowed). Land recently acquired from Mexico would be organized into territories that would decide the issue of slavery for themselves. To please the South, the Fugitive Slave Law was passed, making it easier for owners to have escaped slaves returned.

Violence and Political Debate

The compromise only calmed the situation temporarily. As more western lands were organized into territories, the fight over slavery was carried there. The dispute often erupted into physical violence between proslavery and antislavery groups.

Fit for Servitude

"The worst foes of the black race are those who have intermeddled on their behalf. We know better than others that every attribute of [slaves'] character fits them for dependence and servitude [and] no calamity can befall them greater than the loss of what protection they enjoy under this patriarchal system."

Reverend B. M. Palmer, proslavery campaigner, "Slavery A Divine Trust," 1861

For President
ABRAM LINCOLN.
For Vice President
HANNIBAL HAMLIN.

This banner was used by the Republican Party during Lincoln's campaign for the presidency in 1860. Lincoln's opposition to slavery caused Southerners to fear a Republican victory.

Meanwhile, a new poli[tical] group calling itself the Republ[ican] Party had appeared on the nat[ion]al scene in 1854 and was gai[ning] support. The Republican P[arty] brought together people [who] wanted to abolish slav[ery]. It was opposed by [the] Democratic Party, wh[ich] supported the idea [of] popular sovereignty, [or] the right for states [and] territories to de[cide] slavery issues [for] themselves. In 18[56] Democrat Ja[mes] Buchanan won [the] presidency, [but] the Republi[can] Party grew [in] strength during [the] next four years.

The Election of 1860

The Republican candidate for president in 1[860] was Abraham Lincoln, an Illinois lawyer who had ser[ved] one term in Congress in the 1840s. He had become nation[al]

All One Thing or All the Other

"A house divided against itself cannot stand. I believe this government cannot endure, permanently half slave and half free. I do not expect the Union to be dissolved—I do not expect the house to fall—but I do expec[t] it will cease to be divided. It will become all one thing or all the other."

Abraham Lincoln, Lincoln-Douglas debates, Springfield, Illinois, June 16, 18[58]

known in 1858, when he had challenged Democratic Senator Stephen Douglas to a series of public debates during an election for U.S. senator in Illinois. Although Lincoln lost that election, he had won a large following in the North during the course of his campaign.

White Southerners, meanwhile, were becoming increasingly fearful that a Republican in the White House would mean the end of the southern way of life. There was growing talk in the South of **seceding**, or leaving the United States, if the nation chose to ban slavery.

On November 6, 1860, Lincoln won the election for president of the United States. Southern leaders had warned that a Republican victory would destroy the Union. After Lincoln was elected, leaders in the South decided it was time to act.

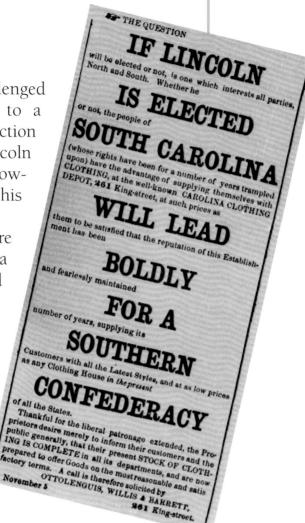

☞ THE QUESTION
IF LINCOLN
will be elected or not, is one which interests all parties, North and South. Whether he
IS ELECTED
or not, the people of
SOUTH CAROLINA
(whose rights have been for a number of years trampled upon) have the advantage of supplying themselves with CLOTHING, at the well-known CAROLINA CLOTHING DEPOT, 261 King-street, at such prices as
WILL LEAD
them to be satisfied that the reputation of this Establishment has been
BOLDLY
and fearlessly maintained
FOR A
number of years, supplying its
SOUTHERN
Customers with all the Latest Styles, and at as low prices as any Clothing House in the present
CONFEDERACY
of all the States.
Thankful for the liberal patronage extended, the Proprietors desire merely to inform their customers and the public generally, that their present STOCK OF CLOTHING IS COMPLETE in all its departments, and are now prepared to offer Goods on the most reasonable and satisfactory terms. A call is therefore solicited by
OTTOLENGUIS, WILLIS & BARRETT,
261 King-street.
November 5

This advertisement published by the Carolina Clothing Depot in 1860 carries a not-so-hidden message. It advertises the latest styles and low prices while at the same time spelling out a warning against the election of Lincoln.

Abraham Lincoln (1809—1865)

Abraham Lincoln was born in Hardin County, Kentucky. He grew up in Indiana and Illinois and, like many farm children, went to school only a few months every year. He educated himself by reading every book he could find. Lincoln learned to hate slavery as a young man during trips on the Mississippi River, when he saw blacks shackled in iron chains, a sight he claimed was "continual torment to me." Lincoln became a lawyer and went into politics in Illinois, winning elections as state legislator and congressman. He was elected president in 1860 and reelected in 1864. He died April 15, 1865, after being assassinated by John Wilkes Booth.

The Threat of War

Breaking the Bond

In 1782, Congress created a Great Seal, the official stamp of the United States of America. One of its inscriptions was "*E Pluribus Unum*"—Latin for "from many, one"—to signify the new unity of the thirteen colonies that had joined together to win their freedom and form a new nation. Southerners were so angry and bitter over the election of Abraham Lincoln in 1860, however, that eleven southern states would break that bond.

This map shows how the states were divided in the early 1860s between those that seceded to join the Confederacy and those that stayed loyal to the Union.

Secession

On December 20, 1860, in South Carolina, 169 delegates to the state legislature voted unanimously to secede from the Union. The reason was simple: South Carolina, one of the states with the highest number of slaves, feared Lincoln would end slavery. South

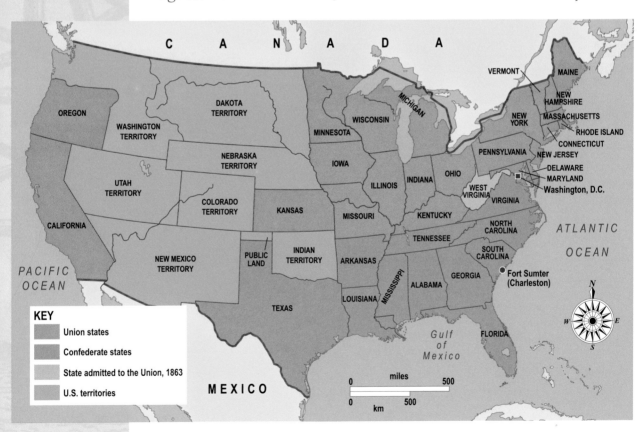

KEY
- Union states
- Confederate states
- State admitted to the Union, 1863
- U.S. territories

People gather on February 18, 1861, for the inauguration of Jefferson Davis in Montgomery, Alabama, the Confederate capital. Richmond, Virginia, became the capital in May after Virginia joined the Confederacy.

Carolinians and most other Southerners believed it was unjust for the North to impose its will on them over slavery. They also feared the move would cripple their economy by denying them cheap labor and lead to violence against whites by freed blacks.

A headline in the *Charleston Mercury* newspaper the next day boldly proclaimed, "The Union is Dissolved." One observer noted South Carolinians were "wild with excitement" about secession and that the sounds of celebration included "church bells mingling with salvos of **artillery**."

Over the next two months, Mississippi, Florida, Alabama, Georgia, Louisiana, and Texas also seceded. On February 9, 1861, delegates of the seven rebel states met in Montgomery, Alabama, and formed the Confederate States of America. As their president, they chose Jefferson Davis from Mississippi, who had resigned his

Fort Sumter

Construction of Fort Sumter started in 1829 as part of a long-term plan of coastal defense begun by the U.S. government in 1817. Named after a military hero, General Thomas Sumter, the fort was located in Charleston Harbor on a small island that the U.S. War Department created in 1829 by

Fort Sumter sits in shallow water in Charleston Harl

dumping tons of granite rubble in a shallow, sandy area. Still under construct when the Civil war began, Fort Sumter was massive. Its brick walls towered o 50 feet (15 meters) high and varied in thickness from 12 feet (3.7 m) at the b to 8.5 feet (2.6 m) at the top. The fort had the capacity for 135 large guns, few were mounted in position when the attack of April 1861 began.

seat as a U.S. senator when Lincoln was elected. Eventually, f more states would join the Confederacy: Virginia, Tennes: Arkansas, and North Carolina.

Reaction from the North

The U.S. government, meanwhile, still hoped to resolve the conf peacefully and preserve the Union. In Congress on December 1860, President Buchanan, still in office until March 1861, said t the U.S. government did not have the power anyway to prev secession by force. On December 18, Kentucky Senator J Crittenden suggested a peace measure that would recognize slav in southern territories, but it was rejected. President-elect Abrah Lincoln and other U.S. officials claimed the southern states had right to secede. Above all, they believed, the Union must stay int

In South Carolina

With South Carolina having seceded, the U.S. military forces in state were in a tricky position. The new South Carolina governm wanted to take over army positions in the state and was negotiat for U.S. withdrawal from those sites. The United States, on

The night of December 26, 1860, the entire Union force in Charleston moved secretly from Fort Moultrie to Fort Sumter, where the soldiers could better defend themselves against an attack.

other hand, had not recognized South Carolina's secession and was not prepared to pull its forces out of the state.

There were four military sites scattered around Charleston Harbor—Fort Moultrie on Sullivan's Island, Castle Pinckney on a small island near the city, Fort Johnson on James Island across from Moultrie, and Fort Sumter in the middle of the harbor entrance. Major Robert Anderson, the U.S. Army commander in Charleston Harbor, had been ordered to defend the forts but not to provoke any conflict. Anderson had only about eighty soldiers of the First U.S. Artillery to guard the forts, and he felt very vulnerable. He knew that if South Carolina forces took Fort Sumter, his soldiers—presently stationed at the small and dilapidated Fort Moultrie—would be overcome.

Moving to Fort Sumter

Fort Sumter had not been readied for action, and its interior was littered with sand and wood from recent construction work. In spite of this, Anderson decided to move his men there from Fort Moultrie because Sumter was stronger, larger, and would be easier to defend. Under cover of darkness on the night of December 26, 1860, Anderson secretly transferred his men to Fort Sumter in rowboats. Also making the trip were forty-five women and children, families of the soldiers.

Southern militia move into Castle Pinckney, until recently a U.S. military post, in December 1860.

South Carolina officials were enraged when, the next day, they discovered what had happened. They immediately seized Castle Pinckney and Fort Moultrie. The Southerners then took over the U.S. **arsenal** in Charleston on December 30 and occupied Fort Johnson on January 2, 1861.

Major Robert Anderson (1805—1871)

Major Robert Anderson was born into a slave-owning family near Louisville, Kentucky. In 1780, during the American Revolution, his father, Major Richard Anderson, had defended Fort Moultrie, the same fort Robert Anderson was in charge of when the Civil War began. After graduating from West Point Military Academy in 1825, Anderson fought for his country several times, including in the Seminole War of 1837. Before the Civil War, he was a teacher at West Point for several years. Anderson retired from active service in 1863. In 1869 he went to live in France, where he died two years later.

Preparing for Battle

Anderson's men were surrounded by thousands of southern **militia**. Together with some loyal civilian workers, the Union began preparing for a fight. Fort Sumter had sixty-six cannons, but only fifteen were mounted and able to fire. The men readied more cannons for battle and strengthened the fort as much as possible against the attack they believed was inevitable.

In January 1861, President Buchanan decided to send two hundred soldiers and some supplies to the fort on a private merchant ship, the steamer *Star of the West*. When the ship arrived in Charleston Harbor on January 9, however, the local militia's cannon fire from the shore forced it to turn back.

Anderson did not fire his own cannons to protect the ship because he was afraid such an action would ignite a war that the Union did not want. The incident greatly angered Anderson, however. He warned South Carolina governor Francis W. Pickens that, if it happened again, Union forces would close the port by destroying any Southern ships that ventured into the harbor. It was a threat Anderson could carry out from his position at Fort Sumter, and it created a tense standoff.

In December 1860, the small Union force in Charleston Harbor raised the U.S. flag at Fort Sumter. It was the beginning of months of uncertainty as the men got ready to defend their fort.

Across the South

After each southern state seceded, its newly created army seized U.S. military installations within its state boundaries. In January and February 1861, forts were taken by southern militia forces from Texas to South Carolina. Two important U.S. facilities in the Confederacy remained untouched because

A large crowd gathers outside the Capitol in Washington, D.C., for the inauguration of Abraham Lincoln on March 4, 1861.

the Confederates did not have ships to attack them—Fort Sum[ter] in Charleston Harbor and Fort Pickens off Florida's coast [near] Pensacola. The nation's attention quickly became centered on F[ort] Sumter because South Carolina was one of the Confederacy's lea[d]ing members. For both sides in the conflict, the fort became [a] symbol of honor as the Union army held firm and the Confeder[ate] forces closed in.

An Oath to Preserve and Protect

"In your hands, my dissatisfied fellow countrymen, and not in mine, is the momentous issue of civil war. The government will not assail you. You can have no conflict without being yourselves the aggressors. You have no oath registered in Heaven to destroy the government, while I shall have the most solemn one to 'preserve, protect, and defend it.'"

President Abraham Lincoln, inaugural speech, March 4, 186[1]

Lincoln Acts

By the time Lincoln was sworn in as president on March 4, 1861, the situation at Fort Sumter had become much more serious. The women and children had been taken back to safety on land, but Anderson's men were running low on supplies and had only enough food to last a few more weeks. Although Lincoln still did not want to fight, the new president realized he had to stand up to the military challenge by the South. In his inaugural address, he promised to defend federal property such as Fort Sumter. He knew that sending aid might spark the war he was trying to avoid, but on April 4, Lincoln nevertheless ordered supply ships to Fort Sumter.

Surrounded

The relief ships Lincoln dispatched, however, would never be of any help. By the time Lincoln acted, the fort was surrounded by thousands of soldiers and more than one hundred cannons that could destroy not only Sumter's thick walls, but any ships that came to the fort's aid. When the South learned of Lincoln's order to re-supply Anderson, Jefferson Davis told the Confederate commander in Charleston, General Pierre Beauregard, to capture Fort Sumter.

On April 11, Beauregard sent three aides to Fort Sumter with a letter demanding the Union surrender. Anderson refused. At 3:20 A.M. on April 12, Beauregard delivered another note. It read: "We have the honor to notify you that we will open the fire of our **batteries** on Fort Sumter in one hour from this time." Anderson shook hands with the Confederates and escorted them to their waiting boat. At 4:30 A.M.—just ten minutes late—Beauregard fulfilled his promise, and the assault on Fort Sumter began.

This photograph of Major Robert Anderson was taken around the time of the attack on Fort Sumter. Anderson was made a brigadier general before he retired from the army in 1863.

The Attack

On Opposite Sides

One of the tragic aspects of the Civil War was how many men fought against soldiers they knew. The emotional and political issues underlying the conflict led old friends, army comrades, and even family members to fight on opposite sides. The battle at Fort Sumter was an example of this. The Confederate officer who gave the order to attack Fort Sumter on April 12, 1861, was Brigadier General Pierre Beauregard. Major Anderson, commander of Union troops in the fort, had taught artillery tactics to Beauregard when the general was a student at West Point Military Academy.

First Shots of the Civil War

The Civil War began with a Confederate shell that exploded harmlessly high above Fort Sumter. It was a signal for the other Confederate batteries to begin a general bombardment.

This map shows the forts and batteries that were dotted around Charleston Harbor in April 1861. Only Fort Sumter was in Union hands, and the Confederates had several points from which to attack the fort.

Cooper River

Charleston

Mount Pleasant

Ashley River

Castle Pinckney

Sullivan's Island

CHARLESTON HARBOR

Fort Moultrie

Fort Johnson

Fort Sumter

Cummings Point

ATLANTIC OCEAN

James Island

miles
0   3
0   3
km

Morris Island

KEY
Forts
Confederate batteries
April 1861

Within twenty minutes, scores of cannon and other artillery pieces that ringed the fort were firing steadily and lighting up the pre-dawn darkness. Confederate soldier D. August Dickert vividly described the continuous firing as "a perfect sheet of flame, a deafening roar, a rumbling, deadening sound." It was all the more dramatic, he said, because it meant, "The war was on." Woken up by the blasts, Charleston residents flocked to the harbor and high points around the city to view the war's first military encounter.

When the attack on Fort Sumter began, many Charleston residents perched on rooftops and climbed church steeples to get a better view.

The First Shot

The question of who fired the first shot of the Civil War has more than one answer. Many accounts say it was Captain George S. James, whose men fired the shell at 4:30 A.M. that exploded above the fort. But because the shot was only a signal for Confederate forces to begin firing, some historians give the honor of unleashing the war's first real shot to Edmund Ruffin. He was a respected, elderly Virginian and an honorary private in South Carolina's Palmetto Guard, a state military unit. The shell that Ruffin fired after the signal was the first shot to strike the fort. Like many historical issues, the question will never be answered to everyone's satisfaction.

The main battery at Fort Sumter had its cannons aimed at Fort Moultrie. The Union soldiers in Sumter began returning fire on April 12, even though their chances of fending off the attack were small.

Besieged Fort Sumter

The **besieged** soldiers in Fort Sumter did not respond for a few hours, mainly because it was still dark and they had run out of oil for their lamps. The first Union shot was fired shortly before 7:00 A.M. by Captain Abner Doubleday (who is also famous as one of the people credited with inventing the rules for baseball).

Anderson and his handful of men faced a hopeless situation on April 12. They were surrounded by some six thousand Confederate soldiers, were low on ammunition and other supplies, and did not know if help would arrive in time. When Beauregard's aides had asked the Union to surrender the night before, Anderson had made a startling admission to the Confederates. He said supplies in the fort were so low that the Confederates could starve them out in a few days without firing a shot. The Confederates decided to attack anyway because they knew Union relief ships were on the way.

During the first day of the assault, Union ships with supplies and soldiers did arrive in Charleston. They would have been destroyed by Confederate artillery if they had tried to land, however, and so they remained outside the harbor, tantalizingly close but of no use to Fort Sumter's defenders.

The First Day

At first, because of inexperience, the Confederate gun crews kept missing the fort, and many of their shots fell harmlessly into the

Pierre Gustave Toutant Beauregard (1818—1893)

Pierre Beauregard was born in Louisiana and graduated second in his class from West Point. Beauregard was considered a hero of the Mexican War of 1846–1848, in which he was wounded in two separate battles. On February 20, 1861, Beauregard resigned from the U.S. Army and joined the Confederate army. In the South, he would forever be known as the "Hero of Fort Sumter" for winning the first military victory of the Civil War. Following his victory at Fort Sumter, Beauregard led troops into battle throughout the war. After the war, he was involved in several businesses, including operating a railroad in Louisiana.

sea. But gradually their aim improved, and cannonballs and explosive shells began battering Fort Sumter.

The Union artillery men inside Fort Sumter began firing back at Confederate batteries, including one at Cummings Point, and other targets such as Fort Moultrie. But the Union counterattack was not very strong because of a lack of manpower and ammunition. There were so few men that they could only regularly fire six cannons. They had no fuses with which to ignite explosive shells and so could only fire cannonballs.

The Confederates, meanwhile, began to heat their shells before firing them—this made them hot enough to set buildings inside the fort on fire. Fort Sumter filled with dense smoke, and

Artillery

The first battle of the Civil War was fought entirely with artillery, the name for a wide variety of large guns that can fire iron cannonballs and explosive shells over long distances. The most common

A howitzer on display at Fort Sumter today.

artillery pieces during the Civil War were cannons. A cannon consisted of a large, long barrel mounted on a solid wooden base. The base usually had wheels so the cannon could be moved easily from battle to battle. Cannons were loaded with single large balls, multiple fragments of metal, or shells filled with explosives that ignited on landing. Civil War artillery included variations on the basic cannon such as the howitzer and the mortar, both of which were short artillery pieces that fired at high angles.

Anderson's small force now had to fight the scorching flames as well as the Confederates.

Although its walls were immensely strong, heavy shells began tearing away huge chunks of Fort Sumter. The bombardment continued all day and through the night, although only sporadically after darkness fell. Anderson's men stopped firing back in order to conserve their dwindling ammunition. To the surprise of soldiers on both sides, no one had been badly injured on the first day of battle.

The Second Day

As dawn came on April 13, the Confederates intensified their **barrages** of shells and cannonballs. After a breakfast of pork and rice, the Union soldiers continued their counterattack.

The massive Fort Sumter began to show signs of wear as the bombardment continued into the second day.

This print, published in a weekly newspaper in April 1861, gives an idea of conditions inside Fort Sumter during the attack.

Pandemonium

"[By noon of April 13] the roaring and crackling of the flames, the dense masses of whirling smoke, the bursting of the enemy's shells, and our own which were exploding in the burning rooms, the crashing of the shot, and the sound of masonry falling in every direction, made the fort a pandemonium."

Abner Doubleday, Reminiscences of Fort Sumter and Fort Moultrie 1860–1861, *1876*

Blazing fires soon became the biggest enemy for soldiers trapped in Fort Sumter. By noon, many sections of the fort were on fire, and the defenders feared the flames could ignite stored gunpowder and shells. Although his men were running low on gunpowder, Anderson had them throw several full barrels of their precious supply into the sea because fires were closing in.

Smoke became so dense in Fort Sumter that the soldiers had trouble seeing and breathing. One private in the fort later recalled that the "only way to breathe was to lay flat on the ground and keep your face covered with a wet handkerchief."

Respect for Brave Opponents

The Confederates were clearly winning, but they respected their enemy because they knew how brave the Union soldiers were and how difficult it was for them to keep fighting despite the smoke and flames around them in the fort. The Confederates even began cheering Anderson's men when they managed to return fire. This admiration was part of their southern chivalry, a code of honor in which soldiers were taught to respect a brave opponent.

Surrender

At 1:00 P.M. on April 13, a shell fragment sent the fort's flag crashing to the ground. Because the Confederates thought Anderson had lowered it in surrender, they stopped firing. When the Union soldiers replaced the flag and Doubleday's gun crew began firing again, the Southerners yelled their approval that their enemy was not quitting.

However, in the brief interlude in which fighting had stopped, a Confederate officer offered Anderson a final chance to surrender. Acting on his own initiative, Colonel Louis Wigfall rowed out to the

On shore, the Confederates kept up a relentless bombardment. At the same time, they cheered their opponents' determination and bravery.

The Confederates raised this flag after the Union surrender in 1861. The Palmetto flag, adopted by South Carolina after its secession, was the first Confederate flag to fly over Fort Sumter and is now on display at the fort.

fort. He climbed into the battered fort, holding a white handkerchief as a sign of truce, and was led to Major Anderson.

Wigfall told the Union commander he had fought bravely but should give up because he could not win. Anderson realized Wigfall was right. "Well, I have done all that was possible to defend this fort," he said. Anderson had the U.S. flag replaced with a white one of surrender. After thirty-four hours of nearly continuous bombardment of Fort Sumter, the first battle of the Civil War ended with a Confederate victory on the afternoon of April 13.

A Tragic Accident

The formal surrender took place at 4:00 P.M. on April 14, 1861. Anderson took the traditional ceremony seriously. His men marched out, he later reported, "with colors flying and drums beating," to the tune of "Yankee Doodle." As a mark of respect for his nation, Anderson ordered his men to fire fifty guns while the U.S. flag was lowered for the last time.

When the forty-seventh gun was fired, a spark accidentally ignited some gunpowder. The resulting

Defending the Fort

"Having defended Fort Sumter for thirty-four hours, until the quarters were entirely burned, the main gates destroyed by fire, the [outer] walls seriously injured, the **magazine** surrounded by flames, and its door closed from the effects of heat, four barrels and three cartridges of powder only being available, and no provisions remaining but pork, I accepted terms of evacuation offered by General Beauregard."

Major Robert Anderson, battle report, April 18, 1861

explosion killed Union privates Daniel Hough and Edward Galloway and injured four other soldiers. It was a tragic conclusion to a battle that had been nearly without bloodshed.

After marching out of the fort they had so bravely defended, Anderson and his men were put on a Confederate vessel that transferred them to a waiting Union ship. They sailed back to New York, where they were welcomed as heroes.

A New Flag over Fort Sumter

When Confederate troops entered the fort, the U.S. flag was replaced with a Palmetto flag, the flag of South Carolina, to the accompaniment of a loud salute from Confederate cannons. (Later, the Confederate "Stars and Bars" flag was raised.) After the takeover of the fort, Governor Pickens gave a victory speech at the Charleston Hotel. Like other people throughout the South, he was jubilant over the victory. "We have humbled the flag of the United States," Pickens boasted. The governor also said he was not worried about the outcome of the war. "Let it lead to what it might, even to blood and ruin," he declared.

Victorious Confederates stand in Fort Sumter soon after the Union surrender. The "Stars and Bars" flying overhead was the Confederacy's first national flag. Fort Sumter would remain in Confederate hands until just before the end of the Civil War.

Chapter 5

The Civil War

Workers in an ammunition factory produce cartridges for guns. During the Civil War, the North was able to provide what its armies needed. In the South, armies struggled for supplies of everything from shoes and blankets to weapons.

Raising an Army

When President Lincoln learned of the attack on Fort Sumter, he realized that the war he dreaded had finally begun. He immediately drafted a proclamation ordering state militias to raise a combined army of 75,000 men to put down the rebellion by southern states. The assault on Fort Sumter enraged Northerners, making them determined to strike back at the Confederacy.

Southerners, meanwhile, were jubilant over the Confederate victory at Fort Sumter. It encouraged more of them to believe not only that secession was just, but that the South could defeat the North. On April 17, 1861, four days after Fort Sumter fell, Virginia became the eighth state to secede. During May, Arkansas, Tennessee, and North Carolina also joined the Confederacy.

The Whole North Became United

"With the first shot against Sumter the whole North became united. Mobs went about New York and made every doubtful newspaper and private house display the Stars and Stripes. When we reached that city we had a royal reception. The streets were alive with banners. Our men and officers were seized and forced to ride on the shoulders of crowds wild with enthusiasm."

Abner Doubleday, Reminiscences of Fort Sumter and Fort Moultrie 1860–1861, *1876*

The Opposing Sides

As the Civil War began, the states were clearly divided between the Confederacy and the Union (see the map on page 16). The Confederacy had 11 states and a population of 9 million people, including 3.5 to 4 million slaves. The Union was much larger—its 22 states had nearly 23 million people. The Union also had wealth, the manufacturing capability to produce weapons, and shipping resources that enabled it to get supplies from other nations.

During the war, the Union army had about 1.5 million soldiers, while the Confederacy had around 1 million. The soldiers who began enlisting after Fort Sumter had patriotic causes to fight for as well as political issues such as slavery. William Thomas of Pennsylvania said he joined the Union army to "go forth in defense of our country's flag that has been trampled in the dust by traitors." Confederate Henry Orr of Texas signed up to "drive the invader from our soil."

The War and Its Leaders

Most of the battles of the Civil War were fought in the South, some areas of which were fought over many times. During brief Confederate invasions, the war also reached north into areas in Maryland and Pennsylvania. It also extended westward to Kansas and Missouri.

During the Civil War, soldiers on both sides were captured and held prisoner by their opponents. This photograph shows Union prisoners held at Castle Pinckney in Charleston Harbor.

Many families lost their homes during the Civil War due to destruction and fighting. This family in the northern United States loads possessions onto a wagon, preparing to flee from advancing Confederate troops.

A Fellow's Feelings

"Presently we got the order to get ready to charge. Can you imagine a fellow's feelings about that time, to have to face thousands of muskets with a prospect of having a bullet put through you? I've heard some say that they were not scared on going into a fight, but I think it's all nonsense. I don't believe there was ever a man who went into battle but what was scared more or less."

Union soldier George Sargent, First New England Cavalry Bugler, journal entry, April 1, 1865

The Confederates had many gifted generals, including Thomas "Stonewall" Jackson, J. E. B. Stuart, and Robert E. Lee. President Lincoln would eventually hand control of the Union army to Ulysses S. Grant, a future U.S. president and able military commander. Several of the Union generals who preceded Grant, however, had little success against the South in the war's first few years.

The First Battle of Bull Run

The first major battle of the Civil War occurred on July 21, 1861, near a small creek in Virginia called Bull Run. When about thirty thousand Union troops headed south to capture the Confederate capital of Richmond, Virginia, they were stopped at Bull Run by Confederates led by General Jackson and General Beauregard, the victorious commander at Fort Sumter. The defeated Union soldiers, hotly pursued by Confederates, fled 25 miles (40 kilometers) back to Washington, D.C.

The Bloodiest Day

In September 1862, Lee, in the first of his two forays into the North, invaded Maryland with a force of 50,000 Confederates. He headed first to Harper's Ferry to capture much-needed supplies, but his main goal was to capture Washington, D.C. In one of the war's bloodiest battles, Union forces led by General George B. McClellan stopped the Confederate advance on September 17. The North had over 75,000 men and the South 40,000, and for a full day they battled between Antietam Creek and the nearby town of Sharpsburg, Maryland. Fighting stopped at dusk, but not before the Battle of Antietam had become the bloodiest single day of the whole Civil

Deadly New Technology

A technological advance in weapons helped make the Civil War the deadliest in U.S. history. The guns and artillery used by both sides were now **rifled**, which means they had grooves in their barrels. This made them far more accurate and far-reaching than older, smoothbore weapons. Military **tactics**, however, were still based on having large formations of men advance on the enemy in the belief that they could get within 100 yards (30 m) of an enemy position before getting hurt. But with the new rifles and artillery, soldiers could hit men as far away as 500 yards (150 m). Because of this, mass charges throughout the war resulted in a terrible death toll for attacking soldiers.

Ranks of soldiers advance into deadly enemy fire at the Battle of Seven Pines in Virginia in 1862.

Abraham Lincoln (third left) reads the Emancipation Proclamation to members of his government before announcing it to the public.

War. The South had suffered 13,724 **casualties** and the North 12,410. The horror of the battle led Lee to comment, "It is well that war is so terrible—we should grow too fond of it."

A New Cause

After Antietam, President Lincoln took the opportunity to do something symbolic and significant. Lincoln was pursuing the Civil War because he believed it was his duty to preserve the Union at all costs. But he had long wanted to end slavery, believing it was morally wrong. On September 22, 1862, encouraged by victory at Antietam, Lincoln announced that, unless the Confederates rejoined the Union by January 1, 1863, he would free their slaves.

On January 1, Lincoln fulfilled his promise by issuing the **Emancipation** Proclamation, which declared all slaves in the South to be free. Although Southerners did not obey the Proclamation by freeing their slaves, Lincoln's act served an important purpose. Lincoln knew that as the war dragged on, Northerners needed a cause to fight for. The war now had two important goals: to preserve the Union and to end slavery. With a new sense of purpose, the Union would slowly but surely overwhelm the Confederacy.

Robert E. Lee (1807—1870)

Confederate General Robert E. Lee is considered the Civil War's greatest military leader. The son of Harry "Light Horse" Lee, a hero of the American Revolution, he was born in Virginia. Robert E. Lee graduated second in his class from West Point in 1829 and became one of the U.S. Army's most respected young cavalry officers. In early 1861, President Lincoln asked Lee to command the Union army in the war that both men believed was inevitable. Because Lee loved his native Virginia, however, he resigned from the U.S. Army on April 25, 1861, and became a Confederate officer. Lee's military skill helped him keep the Confederacy from being defeated for several years. After the war, Lee lived in Virginia, where he became president of a college.

Confederates on the shore try to fight off a Union fleet intent on attacking Fort Sumter (top left) in April 1863, during a long siege by Union forces. At this time, the Union was beginning to overcome the South, but the Confederates inside Fort Sumter held out for nearly two more years.

The North Triumphs

The tide began to turn against the South. The biggest blow came July 1–3, 1863, when the Union defeated Lee in the Battle of Gettysburg in Pennsylvania to end his second attempt to invade the North. In the next two years, the Union's superiority in men and arms began to wear down the Confederacy. The Union won more battles and began repeatedly invading the South.

Fort Sumter during the Civil War

Even before the fighting ended, Fort Sumter had once again returned to Union control. The fort, however, did not fall to Union soldiers in direct combat. During the war, Confederates successfully defended it against several attacks. Its strong, towering walls were mostly reduced to rubble by a twenty-two-month siege that began in April 1863. During the siege, Union ships pounded Fort Sumter with tens of thousands of artillery rounds, but despite the tremendous assault, the Confederates did not surrender. They finally had to leave on February 17, 1865, when the threat of advancing Union troops forced them to evacuate.

In 1864, the Union army under General William T. Sherman cut a destructive path through Georgia, capturing Atlanta on September 2 and then heading on to Savannah. Sherman's invasion came only two months before President Lincoln was overwhelmingly elected to a second term.

The War Ends

On March 25, 1865, Lee's greatly reduced army made one last gallant attempt to attack Union forces at Petersburg, Virginia. But Union soldiers led by General Grant turned the Confederates back, and within a few weeks Lee found himself and his army surrounded.

On April 9, 1865, Lee surrendered. He told his troops that even though they had fought with "unsurpassed courage and fortitude," he had been "compelled to yield to overwhelming numbers and resources." The Civil War, which had ripped apart the nation, was over.

General Lee surrendered to Union General Grant at Appomattox Court House in Virginia. This picture shows the surrender, with Lee (seated left) and Grant (seated center) surrounded by other soldiers.

Conclusion

After the large flag flying over Fort Sumter was shot down on April 13, 1861, Union soldiers raised this smaller storm flag in its place. It is now on display at Fort Sumter for visitors to see.

Testing a Nation's Endurance

"Fourscore and seven years ago our fathers brought forth on this continent a new nation, conceived in liberty and dedicated to the proposition that all men are created equal. Now we are engaged in a great civil war, testing whether that nation or any nation so conceived and so dedicated, can long endure."

Abraham Lincoln, Gettysburg Address, November 19, 1863

No Choice

Historians believe neither President Abraham Lincoln nor Confederate leader Jefferson Davis had much choice in their decisions at Fort Sumter, which led to the outbreak of the Civil War. Davis believed he had to capture the fort to rid the fledgling Confederacy of an enemy within its borders. Lincoln believed he had to defend Fort Sumter in order for the United States to endure and put down a southern rebellion.

Return To Fort Sumter

When Major Robert Anderson left Fort Sumter in defeat on April 14, 1861, he took with him one of the flags that had flown above the fort. On April 14, 1865, Anderson returned with the scorched

Union artillery bombardments destroyed much of Charleston and other southern cities during the Civil War. This is how Charleston looked at the end of the war in 1865.

and tattered flag and hoisted it up a pole to wave proudly once again over the fort. "I thank God that I have lived to see this day," said Anderson. Coming only five days after the South surrendered, the flag ceremony was intended as a symbolic end to the Civil War.

A National Monument

After the Civil War, Fort Sumter was partially rebuilt. In the decades that followed, it was occasionally used as a lighthouse and was manned during the Spanish-American War, World War I, and World War II as a lookout for enemy ships. In 1948, Fort Sumter became a national monument. Although much of the original fort is still in ruins, people today can visit the spot where the Civil War started.

The Legacy of Fort Sumter

The thirty-four-hour artillery duel over Fort Sumter was insignificant in military terms. Yet this minor engagement is better known than almost any other Civil War battle because it was the first conflict of the long, destructive war. The shots fired at Fort Sumter in April 1861 had a momentous effect on the United States. Two halves of the nation, already divided, turned against each other in four years of bloody fighting. Each side became determined to win, and the cost was huge. Not only did the United States pay a high price in human lives, but it took years to rebuild the nation and reconcile North and South.

Time Line

1829	Construction of Fort Sumter begins.
1850	Compromise of 1850.
1854	Republican Party is founded.
1860	November 6: Abraham Lincoln is elected president.

December 20: South Carolina secedes from the Union.

December 26: Union force in Charleston Harbor moves to Fort Sumter.

December 27: South Carolina militia seize Fort Pinckney and Fort Moultrie

December 30: South Carolina militia seize U.S. arsenal in Charleston.

1861 January 2: South Carolina militia seize Fort Johnson.

January 9: The *Star of the West* is turned back as it enters Charleston Harbo

January 9–February 1: Mississippi, Florida, Alabama, Georgia, Louisiana and Texas secede from the Union.

February 9: Confederate States of America is formed and Jefferson Davis is named Confederate president.

March 3: Confederate Brigadier General Pierre Beauregard takes military command at Charleston.

March 4: President Lincoln is inaugurated.

April 4: Lincoln orders relief ships to take supplies to Fort Sumter.

April 11: General Beauregard demands surrender of Fort Sumter; Major Robert Anderson of the Union army refuses.

April 12, 4:30 A.M.: Confederates begin attack on Fort Sumter.

April 13, 2:30 P.M.: Major Anderson surrenders Fort Sumter to Confederate

April 14, 4:00 P.M.: Surrender ceremony at Fort Sumter.

April 17: Virginia secedes from the Union.

May: Arkansas, Tennessee, and North Carolina secede from the Union.

July 21: First Battle of Bull Run.

1862 September 17: Battle of Antietam.

1863 January 1: Lincoln issues the Emancipation Proclamation.

July 1–3: Battle of Gettysburg.

1864 General William T. Sherman leads Union army through the South.

November 8: Lincoln is reelected president of the United States.

1865 February 17: Confederates evacuate Fort Sumter after Union siege.

April 9: Confederate surrender ends Civil War.

April 14: U.S. flag is ceremoniously raised over Fort Sumter.

April 15: President Lincoln dies after being shot April 14.

Glossary

abolitionist: person who supports or works toward abolition of (getting rid of) slavery.

artillery: large heavy guns, such as cannons.

arsenal: storehouse for weapons.

barrage: rapid firing of lots of artillery.

battery: artillery unit that, during the Civil War, usually included between four to eight guns.

besieged: under siege, which is a military operation in which a group of attackers surrounds a target and either attacks it or keeps it trapped in an attempt to force a surrender.

casualty: soldier or other person who is wounded, killed, or missing in battle.

civil war: war between groups within one nation.

civilian: person who is not a member of the armed forces.

confederate: joined together in a confederacy, which is a group of people or states united in a common cause, such as the Confederate States of America. "Confederate" is the term used to describe soldiers fighting for the Confederate States of America during the Civil War.

economy: system of producing and distributing goods and services.

emancipation: freeing; in the 1860s, it referred to the freeing of enslaved African Americans.

legislature: group of officials that makes laws.

magazine: place where ammunition is stored.

militia: group of citizens organized into an unofficial army (as opposed to an army of professional soldiers).

North: northern states of the United States; also used to mean the remaining United States during the Civil War after the other states seceded.

rifled: having spiral grooves cut on the inside of a gun's barrel to make its shots travel farther and more accurately.

secede: withdraw; in the 1860s, it referred to withdrawal from the Union.

South: southern states of the United states; also used to mean the states that seceded and formed the Confederacy during the Civil War.

tactics: science of positioning and moving troops to win a battle.

Union: United States of America under a single government. "Union" is the term used to describe the remaining United States during the Civil War after the other states seceded and to describe soldiers fighting for the Union during the Civil War.

U.S. territory: geographical area that belongs to and is governed by the United States but is not included in any of its states.

Further Information

Books

Bolotin, Norman. *The Civil War A to Z: A Young Reader's Guide to over 100 People, Places, and Points of Importance.* Dutton, 2002.

Douglass, Frederick. *Escape from Slavery: The Boyhood of Frederick Douglass in His Own Words.* Knopf, 1994.

Grant, R. G. *The African-American Slave Trade.* Barrons Educational Series, 2003.

January, Brendan. *Fort Sumter.* Children's Press, 1997.

Marten, James Alan (editor). *The Boy of Chancellorsville and Other Stories.* Oxford University Press Children's Books, 2002.

Web Sites

www.civilwarhome.com/ftsumter First-person accounts and military histories of the attack on Fort Sumter.

www.cr.nps.gov/history/online_books/hh/12/hh12toc.htm Online version of illustrated National Park Service historical handbook about Fort Sumter.

www.nationalgeographic.com/features/99/railroad/index.html Web site offering interactive journeys on the Underground Railroad and follow-up activities.

www.nps.gov/fosu Information and images from the National Park Service to do with Fort Sumter National Monument, which also includes Fort Moultrie.

Useful Addresses

Fort Sumter National Monument
National Park Service
1214 Middle Street
Sullivan's Island, SC 29482
Telephone (843) 883-3123

Index

Page numbers in *italics* indicate maps and diagrams. Page numbers in **bold** indicate other illustrations.

Maryland, 12, *16*, 35, 37
McClellan, George, 37
militia, 21, 34
   see also South Carolina military forces
Mississippi, 11, *16*
Missouri, *16*, 35

North, the, 5, 6, 11, 12, 15, 17, 37, 38, 43
   economy and society in, 7, 8, 9
North Carolina, *16*, 18

Pennsylvania, 12, *16*, 35, 40
Pickens, Francis W., 21, 33

Republican Party, 14, **14**, 15
Ruffin, Edmund, 25

Sherman, William T., 41
slavery and slaves, 5, 8, **8**, 9, 10, 11, **10**,
   12, 13, 14, 15, 16, 17, 18, 35, 38, 39
South, the, 5, 6, 13, 15, 17, 18, 23, 27,
   33, 35, 36, 38, 40, 43
   economy and society in, 7–8, **8**, 9, **9**,
   10, 11, 12, 13, 17
   see also Confederate States of America
South Carolina, 4, 9, 12, **15**, 16, *16*, 17,
   18–19, 21, 32, 33
   military forces, 19, 20, **20**, 21, 25

Stuart, J. E. B., 36
Sumter, Thomas, 18

Tennessee, *16*, 18
Texas, *16*, 17, 21
Tubman, Harriet, 12

Underground Railroad, 12, **12**
Union Army, 18, 19, 27, 34, 35, **35**, 36,
   37, **37**, 38, 39, 40, 41, **41**
   at Fort Sumter, 4, 19, **19**, 21, **21**, 22,
   23, 24, 25, 26, **26**, 27, 28, 29, 30, **30**,
   31, 32, 33, 42
United States, 4, 5, 10, 15, 16, *16*,
   19, 43
   during Civil War, 35, 38, 39, 42
   population of, 6, 7, 10
   territories, 13, **13**, 14, *16*, 18
   War Department, 4, 18
United States military forces, *see* Union
   Army

Virginia, *16*, 17, 18, 36, 39, 41, **41**

Washington, D.C., 11, *16*, **22**, 37
West Point Military Academy, 20, 24,
   27, 39
Wigfall, Louis, 31, 32